UnFriend Her!

Written By

Dr. Kelli Palfy & Dr. Wanda Polzin Holman

Illustrated By

Kyle G. Smith/ @Inkfable

Jenny is 13, but looks like she is 16. Her friends tell her she is pretty, but she struggles to believe it even though she is liked by a lot of the guys in her class. Jenny comes from a great family. Her mother and father run a successful home-based business and although they weren't spoiled, Jenny and her two siblings pretty much got the things they wanted. As a family, they are pretty close... They enjoy Sunday dinners, playing board games and camping together in the summer.

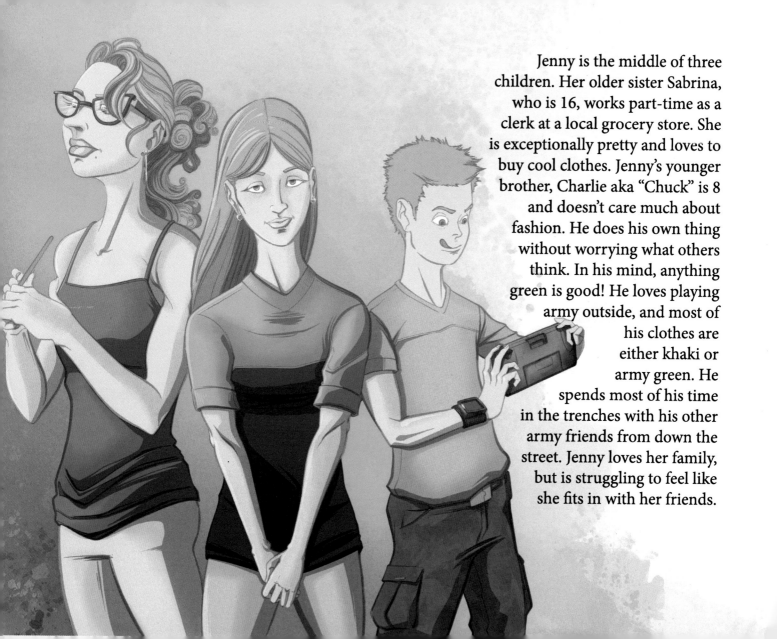

Jenny is the middle of three children. Her older sister Sabrina, who is 16, works part-time as a clerk at a local grocery store. She is exceptionally pretty and loves to buy cool clothes. Jenny's younger brother, Charlie aka "Chuck" is 8 and doesn't care much about fashion. He does his own thing without worrying what others think. In his mind, anything green is good! He loves playing army outside, and most of his clothes are either khaki or army green. He spends most of his time in the trenches with his other army friends from down the street. Jenny loves her family, but is struggling to feel like she fits in with her friends.

Jenny has friends, but things with her best friend have changed. Prior to this year, she and her best friend Mia hung out continually and their age difference didn't matter. Mia is a year and a half older than Jenny, but they grew up together. They lived on the same street their entire lives and both enjoyed a lot of the same things right up until last year when Mia started going to high school.

In high school Mia met several new friends. Although Mia said Jenny was still her best friend, it seemed the two were spending less and less time together as the year progressed. Mia had new friends that she played sports with, worked with at the ice cream shop and did homework with. On social media Jenny would see posts of Mia having fun with others from her 10th grade class who Jenny did not know. They also did things that Jenny wasn't yet allowed to do. Things like going on dates, going to movies without their parents and attending school dances.

Although Jenny was sad, she knew Mia still really liked her, she just didn't have time for her anymore. Jenny didn't want to ruin what they had left of their friendship, so she tried not to let her jealousy get the best of her. She allowed Mia to hang out with whoever she wanted, and tried to pursue other friends herself so she had other people to do things with now that Mia was too busy.

One day, Samantha, who hadn't wanted to be friends with Jenny in the past, approached her at school. Although Sam wasn't typically the kind of girl Jenny usually hung out with, she WAS super popular, so Jenny decided to give her a chance. To her surprise, Sam suggested that they hang out! This seemed weird because Samantha hadn't been very nice to Jenny in the past, once she even bullied Jenny on SNAP. Jenny hoped Samantha's invite was a sign that she'd outgrown her bullying phase. Jenny was lonely and needed new friends so she decided to get to know Samantha better.

That night, Sam asked Jenny to follow her on Insta. A few days later, she approached Jenny again in the girls locker room. She showed Jenny her new leather jacket, which was similar to one Jenny's sister, Sabrina, had just bought. Jenny knew it must've cost her a ton of money and commented on how lucky she was to have parents to buy her such nice things. Sam smiled and told her that she'd actually bought it herself with her own money. She told Jenny that she could help her to make money too…if she wanted. Then she asked Jenny if she wanted to come with her to the school dance in a week… Jenny was both nervous and excited.

Jenny was right! Her parents had noticed that Jenny and Mia had been hanging out a lot less since Mia started high school. They also noticed how depressed Jenny had become and surprisingly said, "YES"! Jenny excitedly began making plans to meet Sam and her friends at the dance. They planned to stay over to Sam's after the dance. Sam told Jenny she was having a 'girls night' after the dance and the plan was to stay up late and watch movies. Jenny wasn't used to staying up late, but she agreed to try!

At the dance, Sam and her friends took a lot of "selfies". Jenny was more sporty than girly-girl and was not used to doing this. She didn't feel particularly comfortable posing for pictures! After the dance, while they were all on their way to Sam's house, Samantha told her that her older brother and a few of his friends were coming over too. Jenny became nervous about meeting him. She knew he was quite a bit older and a football star in college.

When they got there, Jenny was surprised to learn that Sam's parents weren't home. She had presumed they would be. She was also surprised to see Sam and all the other girls' quickly changing clothes and putting on make-up... they began to look like they could be in college too! Jenny enjoyed the dance and survived the selfies but felt anxious and out of place now since she was super sporty herself, and not into make-up.

At Sam's house the girls' selfies got a little more-risky! Two of the girls were pulling their tops up and taking sexy shots. Jenny began feeling super uncomfortable. Sam noticed this and asked Jenny if she wanted a drink to "relax". Jenny's gut-feeling warned her. She was already uncomfortable. Samantha giggled and poured all of the other girls a drink.

When Sam's brother and his 4 friends showed up, each of them instantly "paired up" with one of Sam's friends. They all did shots of alcohol and became louder and louder. The girls got very flirtatious and began posing for pictures for the boys. Sam posed in her fancy outfit and looked like a movie star doing a photo shoot! Two of Sam's girlfriends went with the guys into bedrooms which made Jenny really uncomfortable. Jenny was grateful none of the guys asked her to go to a bedroom with them.

Jenny sat alone and listened to the music and watched everything that was going on. A while later, Jenny saw Sam's brother give her a wad of bills he said was "spending money" from all the guys. He told her that she should split it with all of the girls. Jenny saw Sam count it out and was shocked at how much it was.

Then Sam came over and asked Jenny if she wanted to have some fun posing for pictures too? She said all she had to do was pose and let the guys take pictures of her. She said they were all taking photography classes and that they needed models to practice with. This surprised Jenny because she thought the guys seemed more like jocks than photography types. Nonetheless it sounded harmless, so she agreed.

She posed in her basketball uniform and pretended to be playing. After, Sam gave Jenny some of the money her brother had given her and told her it was "that easy". Sam told her that in the future, if she wanted to make more money, all she had to do was pose for more pictures. Jenny commented that it seemed like the girls who had posed for the sexier photos got more money.

Then Sam teased Jenny about being shy and told her, "yes", that if she wanted to make REAL money, she would have to dress up, look her best, and let the older boys take pictures of her being cute too. Sam picked up on Jenny's nervousness and tried to reassure her that nothing bad would ever happen. She promised Jenny that the guys wouldn't share their photos with anyone.

After the guys left, all the girls wanted to do was sleep. Jenny was disappointed. She'd been hoping to get to know some of the girls better. All the girls, except Ashley, found a couch or bed and crashed. Ashley, who was a bit upset too, left. Jenny had to get up early, so even though she'd planned to stay over, she called her dad to come get her and left too. Her dad asked what had happened, but Jenny didn't know what to say, so she simply said she wasn't able to fall asleep and that she wanted her own bed.

At school on Monday, Jenny saw Ashley, who was also an athlete, in the girls locker room. Jenny asked if they could go for a run together. Ashley agreed and while on the run, Jenny shared what Sam had told her about how easy it was to make money. Ashley said although she didn't enjoy having her picture taken she sure enjoyed being able to buy herself nice clothes.

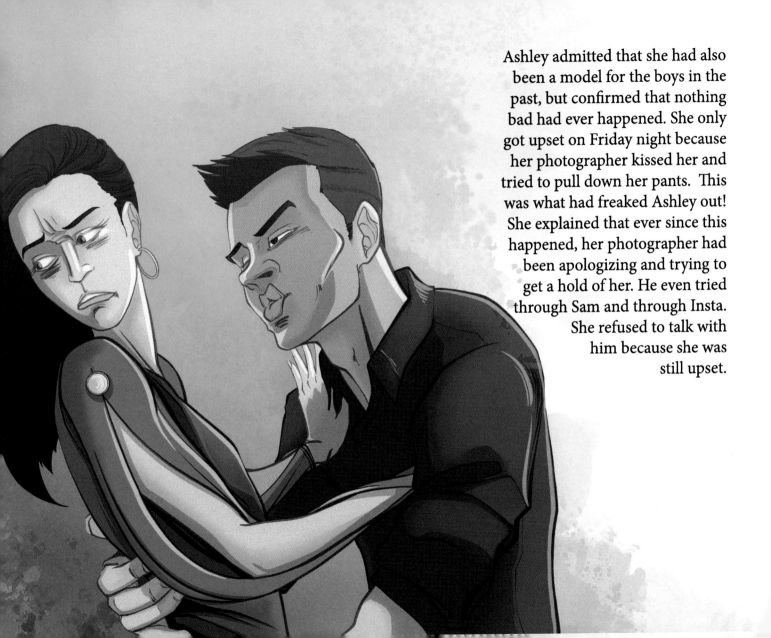

Ashley admitted that she had also been a model for the boys in the past, but confirmed that nothing bad had ever happened. She only got upset on Friday night because her photographer kissed her and tried to pull down her pants. This was what had freaked Ashley out! She explained that ever since this happened, her photographer had been apologizing and trying to get a hold of her. He even tried through Sam and through Insta. She refused to talk with him because she was still upset.

A few days later, Ashley asked Jenny to run again and told her that Joel, her photographer, had gotten her phone number from Sam and was trying to meet up with her. She was starting to get really upset, and didn't know what to do. Jenny suggested she tell her parents, but Ashley didn't want to since she'd lied to her parents about where she was and didn't want to get in trouble.

Jenny told Ashley to DM Joel and tell him to stop contacting her, which she did, but it only seemed to make it worse. He started texting more and insisting they meet. He told her how beautiful she was and that she was a great model, then sent her the most recent pictures he'd taken of her and asked her what she thought. Ashley became sick at the thought of her riskier pictures being 'out there'. At first she thought it was harmless, but now she wasn't so sure.

For the next two days, Joel continued to text Ashley and offered her a lot of money for one last opportunity to take pictures of her. Hoping to make some quick money and then end their relationship, Ashley agreed to meet him and do one more shoot. Then she planned to discuss what he had previously said about not keeping the pictures. Jenny agreed to go with her.

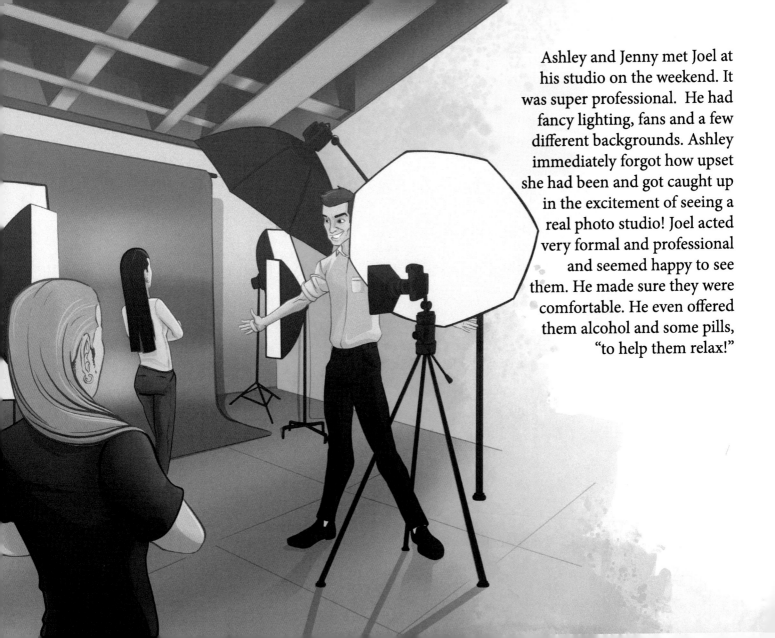

Ashley and Jenny met Joel at his studio on the weekend. It was super professional. He had fancy lighting, fans and a few different backgrounds. Ashley immediately forgot how upset she had been and got caught up in the excitement of seeing a real photo studio! Joel acted very formal and professional and seemed happy to see them. He made sure they were comfortable. He even offered them alcohol and some pills, "to help them relax!"

Ashley took a drink, then changed into the outfit he'd bought for her to wear. This was different than before when Ashley had just worn whatever she wanted. Joel told Ashley that he wanted her to meet an agent and said he would do a professional photo shoot for her tonight. He also told Ashley she would be paid a lot more. Although Ashley liked the idea, the outfit he had brought made her feel uncomfortable. It was very small and didn't cover much of her.

Joel explained that if she wanted to be a professional model, she'd have to prove she was in good shape (meaning she would have to show off her curves). He explained that all models do this and that the photos would be very professionally done. Ashley was nervous, but agreed. It was her dream to be a model. She let Joel take pictures of her from the back when she was topless, and with no bottoms on. Joel thanked her for the pictures, paid her, and told her he would be in touch.

A few days later, Joel texted her and asked her to meet again, to show her the final portfolio. Ashley agreed and met Joel alone. Joel showed her the pictures he had taken. They turned out amazing! But he also showed her some nude photos of other girls, photos that he had taken with a hidden camera from in the washroom! Ashley was shocked! She demanded to know if he had pictures of her like this and insisted he destroy them if he did. Joel said he would have to look. Ashley was horrified and furious. Joel hadn't told her she was being photographed in the bathroom! Ashley left the studio crying and found Jenny.

While she was telling Jenny all that had happened, Joel sent Ashley the nude photos he had taken of her. Then he threatened to post them if she didn't pose for some "even nicer" ones for him. Ashley hadn't planned to pose nude or to meet with him again, but Joel demanded she come alone again the next day. Ashley got really frightened and didn't know what to do, but Jenny had an idea about who might be able to help. She asked if it was ok for her to tell her friend Mia and see if she might know what to do? Ashley agreed, she knew she needed help. She and Ashley met with Mia and told her all that had happened.

Mia's father was a police officer who knew exactly what to do. He seized Ashley's phone as evidence, then arrested Joel for 'producing child pornographic images'. Ashley has NO IDEA this was considered child pornography! The police then seized ALL of Joel's camera and photograph equipment. Mia's father told her he was proud of her for asking for help and for not posing for risky pictures. He told Ashley she was lucky that she hadn't waited even a day longer to get help; that it appeared her photos had not yet been sold or shared with anyone else across the internet. Jenny was mortified at the thought of what could have happened.

Mia's father also told Ashley and Jenny that they had just received a second complaint just like this involving him. They were also told that the young girl involved had been drugged and forced into sexual acts with some of the exact boys that had been at Sam's house! Even worse, it appeared that Sam knew all about it and was OK with it! It seemed like that was her whole intention behind befriending Jenny and Ashley. Both Ashley and Jenny were shaken up by all of this, but grateful that things didn't turn out worse. Both learned a tough lesson that could have ended much worse!

Manufactured by Amazon.ca
Bolton, ON

28485259R00021